I0755975

FINISHING LINE PRESS
www.finishinglinepress.com

Poems for Supper

poemoir by

Leah Stenson

Finishing Line Press
Georgetown, Kentucky

Poems for Supper

ISBN 979-8-89990-514-8 First Edition

ACKNOWLEDGMENTS

A Gift from Greece, Magician and When the Bough Breaks in *vox poetica*
Anniversary and Still Crazy in *River Poets Journal*
Blossoming in Sapporo in *Verseweavers*
Cherry Blossoms in *The Oregonian*
Dance of the Trees in *Gorge Literary Journal*
Honeydew in *Poeming Pigeon*
In the Days of Our First Happiness (originally published as "Changin' Times") in *Triggerfish*
Reconstruction (originally published as "While Repairing a Chimney") in *Eunoia*
Same River Twice and The Garden in *Heavenly Body*
Scenes from a Marriage (excerpted from "Scenes from a Marriage") and Kintsugi in *Life Revised*
Turmoil (originally published as "Untitled") in *The Turquoise Bee*

Publisher: Leah Huete de Maines
Editor: Christen Kincaid
Cover Art and Design: William Stenson
Author Photo: William Stenson

Order online: www.finishinglinepress.com
also available on amazon.com

Author inquiries and mail orders:
Finishing Line Press
PO Box 1626
Georgetown, Kentucky 40324
USA

Contents

For Bill, always…

The course of true love never did run smooth.
—William Shakespeare

Dance of the Trees

I'm waiting for the wild cherries
to tango again like they did last fall
when they dipped and swayed,
trunks wound around one another,
leaves from golden tresses
shimmying to the ground.

I wish the season would linger, forestall
winter winds that strip branches bare,
snow that stills the dance, before
limbs downed by age and ice
are consigned to winter fires.

Let's renounce the warmth of the stove
where we've been firmly planted
watching wood go up in smoke,
shake ourselves loose,
cascade like powdered snow
from the boughs of wind-bent firs.

In the Days of Our First Happiness

The Summer of Woodstock

We shared a second-story apartment
in Binghamton, a rundown college town,
fragrance of lilacs filled our space
through the open bedroom window.

In the evening, we'd drink
a couple of chilled Buds
from Baby Bear Market
and ride to the top of the hill.

On the Fourth of July we threw a party.
Martin distilled ethanol
we mixed with Kool-Aid
in the bathtub.
Everyone was stoned, drunk,
or both, and Barry fell
from the veranda unharmed
into the flower bed below.

A half-century later, we rarely drink
more than a glass of champagne.

These days we get high
on psychedelic sunsets
orchards in bloom
endless starry nights.

Salad Days

What's for supper, you ask.
Poems, I say, *made in a special way.*
I've been at my notebook for hours
whipping up food for thought—
plump tomatoes and hearts of palm,
sweet rolls and half-baked ideas,
succulent oysters on the half-shell
with a bottle of Primavera.
For dessert, wild strawberries,
a cordial and a demitasse.
We'll dine alfresco
gazing at the moon.
You'll be the main dish.

Turmoil

I stumbled through the woods,
chest braced against the wind.
I couldn't love you the way I should,
forgive me for I have sinned.

My need for you tormented me
obscured by clouds I was under.
I hungered for you incessantly,
but was capable only of blunder.

If you love me, pluck a daisy,
not just any flower.
If you don't and think I'm crazy,
demons will my heart devour.

Epic

We lived in a cavernous house
where we couldn't connect.
The rooms were dim in disarray.
You were distant and peripheral.
As I sat down to write a poem,
an eclipse of moths flew in
through the kitchen window.
In my dream, I crossed bridge after bridge
as Buddhists by the side of the road
intoned a prayer to protect me on my journey.
I found myself alone in the Far East.

Reconstruction

You fell like Icarus at the construction site—
fifteen meters to be exact—
eighteen bones broken
and a heart that stopped
three times. But you survived.

Although protected by Herman Survivor work boots,
your Achilles heel was crushed.

Physicians said you might never walk again.
Thanks to the surgeons' skill and good karma,
your heel was reconstructed, broken body mended.

Returning from the shore of the River Styx, you walked
away from your lover in Boston,
flew to Tokyo, back into my life.

Scenes from a Marriage

We resumed our marriage
in a wooden rabbit hutch of a house
without hot running water or flush toilet.
I bathed our daughter by the kerosene stove,
hot water from the ofuro carried in buckets
to the baby's tub on the tatami mat floor.
You came home too late to help.

After our second daughter was born,
we moved into a condo that was haunted.
Doors slammed by themselves
the day we moved out.

In our next house, I waited for you
to come home on the last train
after drinking till late in the yakitoriya,
long after I fed the children
and turned down the lights.

Diagnosed with breast cancer,
I moved back to the States,
leaving you alone
to carry on in Japan.

Persephone's First Spring

A painting evokes a poem—in the foreground flooded with sunlight, a mother pushes her child in a stroller. The child grasps the string of a balloon. In the background, a tunnel to the underworld.

That day in the New York café
my three-year-old let go the string,
her ghost white balloon
leaping beyond reach, pinned
to the hammered tin ceiling.

Her wail stopped the diners cold—
forks frozen midway to open mouths.

Against a tunnel of darkness—
how can one console a child,
a father far away,
mother breaking down,
a strange city,
a flyaway balloon?

Marooned

Our marriage should be on the rocks
with you gone longer than Odysseus.
Having survived Scylla and Charybdis,
you were lured by the sirens' call,
me on my own fending off suitors.
Now you're adrift between
a far-off land and a familiar shore.
I fear your sails are luffing,
your compass broken
and no longer in the gods' favor
you'll be swept away
or return home long after I've departed.
I keep the lantern lit,
keep weaving our story.

Anniversary

Maui

In the tropical Garden of Hana
nothing came between us, joining
the yang of ocean waves beneath the veranda
and the yin of a koi pond at the back door.
That night, a steady rain drenched the earth,
washing clean the years between us.

On the road back from Hana,
you risked the hairpin turns
retrieving cell phone calls
the closer we came to civilization.
By the time we reached Kihei my signal faded.
Only static flowed between us.

Cherry Blossoms

I think of you across the ocean
picnicking under cherry trees
caressed by falling blossoms.

To ponder the impermanence of beauty
you gather with friends and companions
to drink sake and dream.

Far from Tokyo
in a distant land
Spring has passed.

The blossoms here came
and went without ritual.
Gardeners swept them into streets.

Blossoming in Sapporo

After a long cold spell
I was tickled pink
when you invited me to view
the cherry blossoms in Sapporo.

Spring came late to the North.
Snow still lingered in patches
so we took photos of crows
and ate roasted corn instead.

At dusk, plastic flowers danced on wires
across the street from our hotel,
and when we drew close against
the night wind, I blossomed.

Kintsugi

When you chipped the Blue Willow saucer,
I lashed out, swept the joy right off the table.

It takes practice not to dredge up
the times we broke each other's heart.

If we hadn't lived in Japan, could we have learned
the art of joining broken shards with silver, platinum or gold?

Could we have understood the beauty of brokenness,
that nothing is so broken it can't be fixed?

Kintsugi: the Japanese art of repairing broken ceramics with lacquer mixed with precious metals resulting in a new serviceable piece often more beautiful than the original.

Homecoming

You could have been
Shanghaied by Tokyo
leaving me shattered
memories, dashed
expectations,
a trainwreck of the heart.

Instead we're together
morning coffee
blueberry pancakes
robins on the dew-soaked lawn
neighborhood cat
curled up on our doorstep.

Magician

After performing sleight of hand
on the streets of India, you
reward the crowd with pocket change.

You say you can tell a lot about people
by how they respond to magic.
Russians scoff, want you to produce more rubles.
Japanese express restrained amazement.
Italians shout to share the miracle with friends.

Against the backdrop of this mundane world,
where everyone could use more magic,
you perform every day—
to thank a salesclerk who's gone the extra mile,
entertain a distraught child
or simply conjure a smile.

I applaud you.
After you broke my heart
you made it whole again.

Still Crazy

If we had met when you were 50 and
I was 20, we would have gotten on famously.
You would have been my Sugar Daddy and
I would have been the apple of your eye.
Yet, it wasn't in the cards.
Like titans we had to battle it out—
your King Kong to my Godzilla.
Years later, you call me *Honey*,
tell me that I'm *lookin' good;*
I can almost say *I love you.*
Some rush into romance,
others never take the chance.
We've saved the best till last.

Same River Twice

What brings us back to
this neglected Victorian
where we lived as newlyweds?
Will our Russian landlady
who'd now be over 100
still open the door?

Behind the lace curtain
a woman, alone and uncertain,
insists we come back tomorrow.
But we're here now, ready,
having come all this way
just to see where we started.

Your tears and sincerity
allay her fears. She opens the door.
Decades telescope into minutes,
and any doubt you'd love me
to the end is dispelled as we step
again over the threshold.

Honeydew

August moon on the kitchen table
the melon dotted with craters
ripens creamy golden yellow.

A night breeze stirs the air
scent of melon fills the house.

For no particular reason
we light candles on the patio
pop open a split of champagne.

The din of crickets searching
for a mate reminds us of our luck.
Let's wish on Venus, toast
to many more full moons.

Meditation

Inspired by a phrase from C.G. Jung's The Red Book: Liber Novus

For decades, so long apart on different continents,
we shuttled between people and places—
New York, Tokyo, Portland—
our lives blessed with culture, learning, commerce.

At last, together in the abundance
of the edenic Hood River Valley,
we bask in the afterglow of lives fully lived.
In this land of tranquil light
we're *only slightly frightened*
of the oncoming darkness.

The Garden

After years of effort,
the hardscape finally done,
boulders settle like features
in a Chinese painting.

In spring, our landscape boasts
red and green Japanese maples
ornamental blood grass
and creeping thyme.

On rainy autumn afternoons
together behind mullioned windows
we'll write poetry and read it aloud
as wind rattles the panes.

A Gift from Greece

The earrings—
ancient copper
azure patinate
flecked with sun—
whisper your words
in the wind
I am with you.
Even after death,
then, too.

When the Bough Breaks

The neighbor's bull charged into our yard,
used our Japanese maple as a scratching post
and broke many branches. You dug up the tree
and planted another, more perfectly shaped.

Now you're out in the yard in the middle of a snowstorm
fashioning crutches out of wood and twine
propping up the new maple's branches,
determined to protect it from destruction.

I pray you won't be over-protective
when the time comes for me to leave,
that you'll let me be that red maple adorned with snow,
let me bend and break with the weight of it,
go with the natural flow of things.

Leah Stenson is a poet, editor and memoirist whose writing explores themes of trauma, healing and transformation. Her memoir, *Life Revised* (Cirque Press, 2020), chronicles her journey from childhood grief to spiritual renewal, guided by her 50-year Buddhist practice.

Originally from Long Island, Leah worked as an assistant editor in New York City before spending sixteen years in Tokyo studying Japanese, teaching English as an adjunct lecturer, and raising a family. After returning to the U.S. in 1993, she settled in Portland, Oregon where she served for several years as Managing Director of Oregon Peace Institute. It was in Portland that she found her creative community and began writing poetry.

In addition to *Life Revised,* Leah authored three books of poetry—*Heavenly Body, The Turquoise Bee and Other Love Poems,* and *Everywhere I Find Myself*—and co-edited the award-winning anthology *Reverberations from Fukushima: 50 Japanese Poets Speak Out* and served as a regional editor for *Alive at the Center: Contemporary Poems from the Pacific Northwest*. She also served on the boards of several literary and cultural organizations. Leah continues to promote poetry as the host of the long-running Studio Series Poetry Reading and Open Mic. For more information about Leah and the Studio Series, see *www.leahstenson.com/blog.*

www.ingramcontent.com/pod-product-compliance
Lightning Source LLC
LaVergne TN
LVHW090542110826
845146LV00003B/1229

* 9 7 9 8 8 9 9 9 0 5 1 4 8 *